Discovering Madrid

Ana Campoy

Roser Calafell

laGalera

"Grandpa, we are in Madrid!"
"Finally, you came indeed!
With the help of this map
we'll get everywhere in a flash.
There's a lot to see, we have to rush!"

"This monument is very old
but also big and bold.
Through the Puerta de Alcalá
entrance to the capital was gained."
"Look at it, it's beautifully maintained!"

“Grandpa, buy me a balloon”
“Not now, we don’t have any room!
In this square you can buy
stamps, silver coins...
or a yummy sandwich, oh my!”

The bells of this clock
bring us good luck
when they welcome the new year.
"Lola, look at the ground:
starting from here the roads go all around!"

"Don't you think this statue has lots of flair?
It's a beautiful lady bear"
The balloon starts to fly.
"Oh no! Catch it grandpa!"
"Look at it: from Madrid to the sky!"

"This painting is so grand!"
"Looking at the Prado's pictures
you'll travel to a faraway land.
Pablo, think about your balloon:
it will explore the Earth and the Moon!"

NDIA
COCINA HINDÚ
ESPECIALIDAD
TANDOORI

"Having some wine and tapas
you can even see the chulapas.
A cocido is fit for a Queen
but I'd like to lick my fingers clean
with a curry in Lavapiés today!"

A very special little mouse
at calle Arenal has its house.
Like the Tooth Fairy, he keeps the teeth
he collects from all the kids.
"Yum, yum... hot chocolate!"

FACTORIA
RATONIL
Pérez
Casa Museo del ratón Pérez
Casa Museo del ratón Pé

At El Retiro park you can always
roller skate on its pathways.
"The Palacio de Cristal
you and your friends will enjoy"
"To the rowboats, sailor boy!"

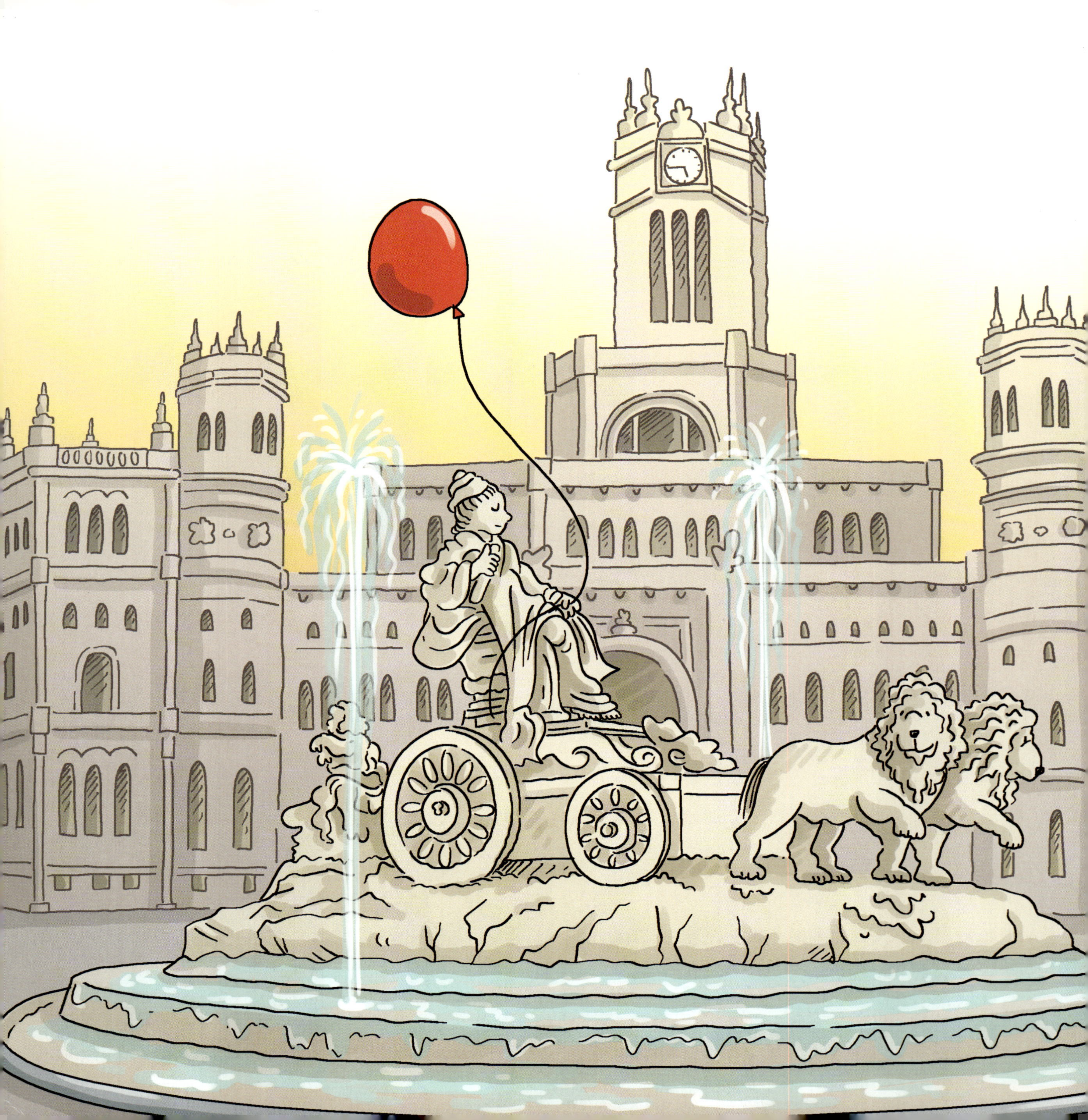

"When I get to Cibeles square
I can feel the joy is in the air.
"She is our crowning jewel
and we love her like a treasure
"My balloon –what a pleasure!"

We arrive in this occasion
at the end of our presentation.
At Gran Via's theatre row
they are all ready to start the show.
"This was sublime!"
"Come back soon another time!"

Cines Callao
Schweppes

"To Nicolás y Sofía,
for their upcoming visits to Madrid".
And to my grandfather Jesús, "el madrileño".

First published in Spain in May 2014 by La Galera Editorial

English version: Yolanda Porter

La Galera, SAU Editorial
Josep Pla, 95. 08019 Barcelona
www.lagalera.cat / lagalera@lagaleraeditorial.com
facebook.com/editoriallagalera
twitter.com/editorialgalera

Printed in Talleres Gráficos Soler
Enric Morera, 15. 08950 Esplugues de Llobregat

Printed in UE
Legal deposit: B-5.855-2014
ISBN: 978-84-246-5227-2